Moon Dance

JAN NEWHOUSE

Moon Dance
LIFE THROUGH THE CANCER LENS

A portion of the proceeds from the sale of this book goes to The Wellness Community of Greater St. Louis, the St. Louis Cancer Foundation, and the Susan G. Komen Foundation.

Published by Arvey Publishing, P. O. Box 220040, St. Louis, Missouri 63122
http://www.moondancebook.com
e-mail: info@moondancebook.com

ISBN:0-9755731-0-1

Printed and bound in the United States
Cover Photograph by Dan Dreyfus
Book Design by Georgia Schmidt

FOR PAUL AND JULIE
The brightest stars in my universe

Acknowledgments

This book is dedicated to Dr. Susan Luedke and Dr. Julie Wiehl, who listen with the heart as well as the stethoscope, and to Inge Hynes, Bruce Schmidt and Mary Mondello, who provided light when I needed it most. Deepest thanks to the nurses and staff at the St. Louis Cancer and Breast Institute, my second family, whose love and caring know no limits.

Artistic thanks to Marty Clarke, P.A., Rudy Willis, M.D., and musician Brian Clarke whose creative projects produced a synergy that took us all to higher levels. Thanks to Dan Dreyfus and Marty Clarke for their exquisite photographs, and to my graphic designer, Georgia Schmidt.

Novelist George Eliot said, "My friends are the well-spring of my life." It is impossible to mention all those loving friends who have seen me through 15 years on the cancer roller coaster. Forgive me if I miss your name. Heartfelt thanks to my closest friend, Suellen Meyer, who stood by me every step of the way. Deepest thanks to my personal support groups of Kathy and Lisa; Sharon, Maggie and Janet; Karen, Connie, Ethel, Kitty and Sue; my JBS friends, especially Margaret and Becky; Peter & Madelyn; my Ann Arbor stalwarts Marta, Persie, Julie & Rick, Verena, BJ and the Chelsea group; Barb from Share; Jane and her sons; and the Brighton contingent, especially Lynne.

A special thanks to our *Stage 5: Staying Alive Club*—Suzie, Debbie, and Wendy—whose courage and caring continue to inspire me, and to Wendy O. and Scott Los who showed me miracles are possible.

Thanks to Michael Morrah and Janice Cannon for their generous professional services on this book, to The Wellness Community and The St. Louis Cancer Foundation for urging me to publish, and for the personal support of Mark Travis and Lisa Wiley.

As one who thrives near water, thanks to Barcy and Carl Fox whose stimulating conversation and retreats on the Current River and in Cambridge inspired many poems; to Sharon and David who shared the wonders of dolphins, pelicans, shells and sea on the Outer Banks; and to my aunt Sue, brother Tom, sister Cathy and her family, and my mother Helen for life and love on the Pacific. My poems emerge with the waves every summer on Lake Michigan, where Paul, Julie and I celebrate being a family.

Appreciation to Chris and Jan at YogaSource and Lyn and Kitty at Big Bend Yoga who helped me decrease pain and seek integration. Also thanks to Jan Cannon and the wonderful participants—Carol, Kay, Stephanie and many more—in the Women's Career Development Program at Meramec Community College, my teaching colleagues in Boston and St. Louis, and in tribute to Mary Paffrath, a beacon of hope.

A final heartfelt thanks to Marty Clarke who believed in me and made this book happen.

I am humbled by the richness of my world.

Jan

Preface

Don't be afraid of these poems. No English teacher will swoop down to quiz you about muddled metaphors or obscure symbolism. My poems come straight from the heart.

This book evolved from my experience with cancer. Any life-threatening disease changes your world forever. Colors become brighter; experiences more intense. Emotions bounce all over the spectrum as you try to redefine your identity, your relationships with others, and your value and place in the world. Time takes on a new urgency. Cancer colors every part of your world, even your dreams.

Unlike reading a novel where you must start at the beginning, a collection of poems and photographs invites you to skim happily and stop to nibble any poem or photograph that catches your eye. Like a collection of fine chocolates, some of my poems are nutty and funny; some creamy and full of flavor; while others require rigorous chewing for full effect. And for those few who dislike poems or chocolate, short narratives and stories are sprinkled though the book like apples, strawberries, or kiwi. Flavors exist for every palate.

My poems highlight some concerns common to all cancer survivors, moving from the *Darkness of Diagnosis* to the *Transformation of Inner Light*. Some people emerge stronger from the caldron of cancer, while others are consumed by it. A medical cure is not always possible, but integration or healing may be.

The extraordinary talents of Dan Dreyfus and Marty Clarke glow in the photographs in this book. Some poems were inspired by and written for specific photographs. Other photos were chosen to create a mood for a section and to challenge the reader's senses and creativity. Marty's words embrace this synergy: "Poetry and photography capture emotion and beauty as they intersect with life."

People ask why I write about cancer. It's because I can't *not* write about it. The overwhelming emotions of fear and hope before a CT scan, the intense grief when a cancer friend dies, the life-giving closeness of family and friends—all need to be processed. Poems condense great feeling into a few lines and help me discover and name what I'm feeling and gain a small sense of control.

I also write to reinforce community, first during the support group years and later—when I was diagnosed with metastasis—for the community of my medical caregivers. Ironically, as my prognosis deteriorated, the more I turned to humor and a realistic optimism to combat it. Once, after a beloved patient died, one of my chemo nurses said, "We need a poem." To me that was the highest honor. At times, the pen is mightier than the scalpel.

Some final thoughts: These poems were written over a seven year period and are not arranged chronologically except for *Shadows and Light*. Some of the poems in *Darkness,* for example, were written at the time of diagnosis; others when I learned I had metastasis; and others were written this year. While the book overall moves from darkness to light, each section contains a variety of writing styles and moods, including humor, which can make the pain more bearable. I feel vulnerable disclosing my emotions and experiences, but if any of these poems move you or give you new insights or perspectives, the risk will be well worth it.

Contents

DARKNESS

Facing diagnosis, isolation and loss

In the second when the words "You have cancer" leap from the doctor's lips to your ears, a deep abyss opens where once there was solid rock. Although the world looks the same on the outside, for you it will never be the same again.

For me the date was October 23, 1987. I was 42 years old with a husband and a young daughter—and I was absolutely terrified. I didn't fit any of the risk categories and was shocked when my routine mammogram showed a suspicious lump that turned out to be cancer. I followed the traditional treatment at the time: mastectomy with 16 lymph nodes removed (2 positive for cancer) followed by 6 months of chemotherapy (Cytoxin, Methotrexate, 5FU). I found denial a great coping mechanism, so I kept working from my hospital bed as if nothing cataclysmic had happened. But something important had happened—as these poems express. Cancer impacts every area of your life from physical appearance and emotional upheaval to self-image and personal relationships.

My cancer journey, which seemed to be over in 1988, returned almost 10 years later as breast cancer metastasis in 1997. Although uncertainty rules the world of cancer, there was one certainty for me from the day of first diagnosis: I would do everything in my power to live until my young daughter was old enough to thrive on her own.

The Waiting Room

They come, these implacable tears,
As I sit in the crowded room,
waiting for the results of my tests.

A woman coughs, sprinkling germs on us like sugar on a donut.
My ears mute the other sounds around me,
Isolating me as I wait...and wait...
For the perky nurse
Who chats me into the examining room.

The air is always cold in here.
My paper gown rustles stiffly when I move.
I glance out the window at the gray sky.
I look at the metal instruments aligned on the table.
I stare at the poster of a skeleton that never changes—
Even as my own falters.

Faint noises hum outside my chamber,
Doors opening and closing.
Nurses shouting to deaf old men,
"Just wait, Mr. Jones. The doctor will be here soon."

"The doctor will be here soon."
Those words ring like a false mantra.
There is no "soon" in a doctor's office.

I stand and stretch,
Leaf listlessly through a magazine.
Shouldn't I be next?

Finally the telltale signs—
The sounds of files being snatched from the door
Some fumbling at the doorknob
The doctor gliding in, glancing at my charts,
Not yet making eye contact.

Will it be today I hear bad news?
Or next month? Or the month after that?
I sit
And I wait.

Diagnosis

When the doctor says "malignant,"
The words bypass your ears
Bypass your brain.
"Will I live? Will I die?"
"Will I live? Will I die?"
Pulses through your veins.

Your blood pressure soars.
While the doctor drones on about drugs,
You think only of basics:
What will my husband say?
My mother?
Oh God, my child! How will I tell my child?

Panic paralyzes you.
"Are you okay?" asks the doctor
As if "okay" will ever be part of your vocabulary again.
"I…"
"How long will I…?"
"Will I…?"

The word "live" can't make it past your lips.
The journey from heart to head is so twisted and arduous,
You can't ask the crucial question.

You bury your face in your hands.
"Is there someone I should call?" the doctor asks.
The dead weight of your head nods "no."
There is everyone and no one to call.

You have cancer—in your breast today,
Perhaps in your bones tomorrow.
They call it breast cancer, but you know better.
The place that really hurts—
Is your heart.

Into the Valley of the Shadow
The Valley of the Shadow
Valley of the Shadow
Of the Shadow
The Shadow
Shadow

Cards

Some days Cancer holds the cards.
You sit there beaming
With 2 kings and 2 queens
Desperately trying to keep a poker face.

Cancer antes in.
Your counts are good.
You've been exercising regularly.
You've even eaten shark cartilage.
So you put in 10 dollars and raise the stakes.

Cancer meets your bet and raises 5.

You start to sweat as you draw your last card:
A king! A full house!
Backed by all that royalty
And the power of Adriamycin and Taxol,
You look Cancer straight in the eye and raise 5 more.

The crowd is rooting for you:
Your friends and family
Your doctors
Your support group
Your chemo nurses
All wait eagerly.

Cancer calls.

Triumphantly you lay down your hand:
Regal kings and queens. A royal full house!
You lean back, cloaked in confidence.
You've played this game as well as you could.

Cancer pauses—and then shows its hand—
Turning ace over ace over ace.

You fold.

They Mean Well

"Have a positive attitude."
"I already do. I'm absolutely positive I hate cancer."

And the Oscar for the
Worst Supporting Behavior
from Well-Meaning Friends…

No one knows exactly what to say to a new cancer patient, and sadly, some people you love drop by the wayside…

Faculty, students and staff at the college I worked for were extremely supportive when they heard of my cancer, turning my hospital room into a floral shop and keeping postal workers inundated with cards. When I recuperated from my operation and returned to my position as Director of the fledgling Women's Career Development Program, I completed arrangements for our first graduation ceremony, inviting the college president to give the keynote address. As we stood in the wings chatting, right before I was going on stage, the president said, "I hear you've started chemo. I've always wondered. What does it feel like with all those IVs and things? Is it painful?" I couldn't believe my ears! Here I was, trying to be a professional not a patient, and he brings up the scary specter of chemo as a conversational gambit. Ignoring his question, I gave him a smile and then walked on stage to the life I preferred.

My friends are very well-intentioned, but two of them sent me the same book on how to beat cancer with positive thoughts. Reading the book, I realized that if you can miraculously "cure" your cancer through a positive attitude, then conversely, your bad attitude could cause cancer. Did my thoughts somehow cause my cancer? And if so, which thoughts? Guilt rained over me that somehow I might be responsible for my disease. I felt anger at those who exposed me to this view, particularly while I was going through the caldron of cancer. It took a long time and some scientific breakthroughs (identifying the BRCA gene that carries cancer or the effect of Herceptin to neutralize my HER2/neu, for example) before I could shed this irrational cancer guilt. I heard a line on an audiotape that finally set me free. "You can't give yourself cancer," the speaker said. "You're just not that good!"

❖   ❖   ❖

My first day back in the English department was someone's birthday, so we all gathered for cake and singing. I got lots of hugs and felt great being back. One crusty old professor turned to me during a conversational lull and said loudly, "My wife had breast cancer and had a lumpectomy. No one needs to have a mastectomy anymore." In the sudden, uncomfortable silence, rather than defend my medical decisions to a rude old man, I joined my friends and had another piece of cake.

❖   ❖   ❖

My husband was very supportive during my cancer, doing the grocery shopping, vacuuming the house, or holding and hugging me when I was feeling down. He's a very honest man and would not say things he didn't know to be true, like "Everything's going to be fine." I considered this a deficiency since I wanted reassurance—until I saw what happened to other women with cancer. One woman's husband started a blatant affair, leaving a trail of hotel credit card bills. When confronted, the husband announced he was just looking for what his wife couldn't provide right now. Another husband moved out altogether. "It's too depressing to live with a cancer patient," he told his wife. Another cancer patient's mother could not handle the strain of cancer. Every time her adult daughter tried to talk about it, she would change the subject. Finally realizing communication was impossible, the daughter capitulated. At the end of each conversation her mother would say, "And you're doing fine. Right?" "Yes Mom, I'm doing fine."

Sex

With cancer,
Sometimes your sex life
Is shorter than
a poem.

I Want my Estrogen Back!

So, what's the problem here?
I want my estrogen back!
That wonderful hormone that makes me notice
The broad shoulders of a man's body
And the muscles streaming down his arms and legs.
That hormone that makes furtive glances exciting
And adds a flirting edge to conversation.
Where is that elusive creator of those mysterious fluids
And arousing scents which make encounters possible?
I want my estrogen back!
Now!

Loss

Let it drip from your body
This pain
Until it rains from every pore.

Tears?
      Those are for the lightly wounded
      Easily shed
      Easily forgotten.

For you, the rivers and oceans:
The torrent of wave upon wave
Crashing on the battered shore.

And each time you think it's the last,
A stronger wave strikes you unaware
Drawing you deeper into the dark, gray sea.

Paper Doll

I entered the examining room this morning
With strong body lines
A heft to my step
And a smile in my voice.

When my doctor explained that my bone scans
Were not good and I'd need to start chemo,
My backbone began to crumble.
My body deflated like an old balloon.

As the doctor talked, I tried to listen
But I was becoming transparent.
Sounds went through me without registering.
My head nodded as if I were listening,
But it was as flimsy as a paper doll's.

The wind wafted me out of the office
As gently as a kite cradled in a summer breeze.
My body became lighter and translucent:
No head, no heart, no bones to anchor me to the earth.

By the time I reached the parking lot,
I was two dimensional,
Shedding my human side
To survive in a cancer world.

Glance

Walking by the window
I glimpse a quick reflection in the glass:

A woman's gaunt face
Dark circles sagging under listless eyes
Patches of hair thinning or gone.
That can't be me.

So I slowly lower the blinds
And turn the television on.

Glass

When they told me my cancer came back,
I broke glass.

I packed a box of old bottles
And drove to the recycling center:
Carefully selecting a long green wine bottle,
I hefted it in my right hand like a quarterback
And threw the bottle with all my might.
Crash!!!
Glass hit glass: raining deadly shards
On the other bottles in the bin.

Quickly I picked up another bottle—
And another and another—
Until the crashing was constant and flying shards reigned in the air—
A sibilant symphony of destruction.
I was so enthralled,
I didn't even notice the tears streaming down my face.

By the time I picked up the last bottle, I was spent.
I tossed it over the wall like an afterthought.
Exhausted, I put the empty box in the car and drove home,
Leaving my anger in a million jagged pieces.

Deep

In the winter, I go deep
Sending my spirit into the frozen caverns within me
Where memories are buried and imaginings are real.

As the days grow shorter
I seek the shadows within myself.
My own darkness speaks without language:
A primitive calling to those deepest chambers
Of myth and memory.

As the earth tightens its revolution around the sun
I find strange comfort in that shadow world
Where birth awaits
And sun is just an illusion.

In the winter, I go deep.

SHADOWS AND LIGHT

Seeking connection through support groups

Emerging from the fear and darkness of diagnosis is not a steady journey. Like waves, you wash in toward the comfort of shore only to be pulled back into the shadows of the sea. Most patients find a source of light to guide them—nature, family, friends, faith, a trusted doctor, an intense life spirit, an Internet chat room, a sense of community—the sea surges with possibilities.

When my cancer returned in 1997, I needed every bit of help I could get. I discovered that a support group led by a licensed facilitator provided friends who were facing similar challenges, and offered not only emotional support but also practical ideas to face the caldron of chemo. This section contains the poems I wrote while in a support group and contains the stories of my peers—who provided light when I needed it most.

Support Groups

The poems in this section are dedicated to The Wellness Community support group facilitator, Inge Hynes, and to all those courageous group members, past and present, who laughed, loved and cried together as they battled cancer and fought their way toward healing. Not all of them lived, but each came to terms with the illness and achieved wholeness.

I am absolutely not a support group person—or so I thought. I've always been introspective, independent and outspoken—and I like to be in control. As I discovered, cancer likes to be in control, too.

So, when first diagnosed with breast cancer 15 years ago, I conducted business from my hospital bed and kept in close contact with my students. Letting cancer know it wasn't going to destroy my life, I thought was being realistic. Friends immediately saw *Denial* written all over me.

I didn't consider a support group then because I feared meeting people suffering or dying from cancer. Instead, an organization matched me up with Barb, a cancer survivor my age with small children, who immediately empathized with my fears for my own child. The telephone was my lifeline as Barb helped me through the frightening times before scans and tests until I was "cured."

After ten cancer-free years, my cancer returned in my bones and then liver. I trembled just hearing the word "liver." The fear of death paralyzed me. Several research studies showed that cancer patients who participated in support groups lived significantly longer than those who did not. Eager to use every resource available, I took the plunge and joined a weekly support group at

The Wellness Community of Greater St. Louis, one of the best experiences of my life. Far from being depressing, the group used listening and empathy to create a climate where disclosure was possible and deepest fears could be discussed. We taught each other to be proactive in our medical treatment, deal positively with family problems, and face our fears and loss. But most of all, we became a family.

Our group of 12 included a witty waitress; a lawyer whose cross-examinations produced insight; a nun who smoked marijuana to control nausea; a widowed grandmother courted by an old high school beau; a young mother with two children, a caterer, a counselor, a teacher, a Food Bank volunteer, a medical worker who offered rides to group members…you name it. Despite the variety of ages, jobs, ethnic backgrounds, and socio-economic status, our common enemy—Cancer—broke down all barriers as we became a family.

Laughter and tears prevailed in even measure. We affirmed each other's feelings and could talk about those emotions and fears we couldn't share with our spouses or children—feelings that only another cancer patient could understand. We shared the joys of participants who "graduated" from group when they were cancer free, the sorrow of those few who died, and the day to day support to keep us strong. For me, it was literally a lifesaver.

The Wellness Community also offers support groups for families, friends, and caregivers who have different issues to explore. The amazing aspect of The Wellness Community is that all services from support groups with licensed facilitators to educational presentations, stress management programs and gentle movement classes like yoga are provided at no cost to cancer patients. The National Wellness Community, with facilities across the United States, has a web site at www.thewellnesscommunity.org.

Thoughts on the First Day of Wellness Group

The intensity was palpable
As I sank into pillows
Surrounded by chair:
An island refuge in a sea of new faces.

I watched and waited.
What unwritten rules and rituals?
What stories and sadness behind those smiling faces?

Would I talk?
Would I disclose?
Could I tap the rhythms dancing in my head?

Ritual pacified me.
Women said their names proudly
Easing gently into a practiced litany:
Describing their illnesses by rote
Taming their demons by naming them.

The listening was intense.
Women leaned closer,
Watched with the heart's eye,
And listened as my own words tumbled out
Trembling, awkward, insecure.

Their laughter delighted me.
I feared a group bound to depression and despair.
Instead a stubborn courage
An opening to healing
A fountain of feeling flooded the room.

I knew these women:
          Not yet their names
          Not yet their faces
          Not yet their stories
Yet I knew them
And in this deep connection
I found I could be strong.

Used Parts

Time to take inventory in the used parts department.
Time to take pen in hand and count the missing limbs:

> 5 full breasts (one C cup)
>
> 2 whole kidneys (more than enough for beef and
> kidney pie)
>
> 2 portions of lung (slightly discolored)
>
> A complete set of reproductive organs (hardly ever used
> except on weekends)
>
> And a small basket of lumpectomies and lymph nodes
> in all shapes and sizes.

Time to admit these are just not going to sell.
I guess it's time to write them off:
Human Depreciation.

Act III

Will I leave support group like Andy
Both feet on the ground
Striding into a new life?

Or will I leave like Sue
Who used to bound up the stairs
Eager to attend group—
Until the steps became higher and harder
And she needed to use the elevator.
From there it was just a short step
To walking with canes.
And even shorter still
To being pushed in a wheelchair.

Finally,
Only the voice was left.
But oh, what a voice!
Valiantly whispering in conference calls
Remaining part of the group.

Then there was silence.

But each week, Sue's voiceless presence
Eloquently speaks to each of us:
Showing us how to live fully
And, when it is time, how to die.

The Harvest

You've heard the story a dozen times:
They sewed her up.
The doctors operate
And find a lump the size of an orange, say,
Or a walnut or a cantaloupe.
Why not the size of a tennis ball?
Or a bicycle?
As if any of these objects belonged inside her.

And so they sewed her up.
Because that orange or walnut or cantaloupe
Sent out tendrils
Twisting and weaving around kidneys and colon
Like ivy insidiously clinging to an old Gothic building.

And so they sewed her up
And sent her home—
With that orange or walnut or cantaloupe inside—
To watch the hour hand and then the minute hand
Move round and round the clock,
While that strange garden continued to grow.

But this the doctors forgot:

> *Soul can melt steel*
> *Hope can tame terror*
> *Faith can breed strength.*

And so they sewed her up
But the best parts—
The heart, the head and the soul—
Endure.

Tantrum

"It's my turn!"
I wanted to shout
As women spoke of deep and serious matters
While I sat invisible on the couch.

It's my turn!
I squirmed on the cushion
Aching to tell my happy news—
But the others kept on talking.

It's my turn!
I fumed, looking at my watch,
Knowing the time was almost up.

It's my turn!
But I know my meager news
Could not be squeezed
Into this somber session.

It's my turn!
But I'm no longer there:
Erased, discounted, a mote of dust on an empty shelf.

So I've gone to my room to sulk.
It was my turn, too.

Menu

Inge gives us soul food.
Her words comfort us
Like tomato soup and grilled cheese
On a rainy day.
Or macaroni so thick and creamy,
It coats our fears
With a life-affirming sauce.

Her recipe for group sessions
Is peppered with sage comments,
Salted with gasps of surprise
(Did your doctor really say that?)
And blended together with lots of TLC.

No, you won't go hungry at Inge's Café.
A steady diet of her stick-to-the-ribs cooking
Can help you face chemo, radiation,
CAT scans and transplants.

So, place your order today.
A master chef is at work.

Right Now

I don't feel the cancer
Right now
I don't need hard chemo
Right now
I don't like to be reminded
Right now
That my cancer may be spreading
Right now
May be attacking vital organs
Right now
May be changing my life forever
Right now.

So I go to other groups
Right now
To work and to yoga
Right now
To lunches with old friends
Right now

And forget—for just a moment—

> *Tomorrow may bring Adriamycin*
> *Tomorrow may bring hospitalization*
> *Tomorrow may bring another friend's death.*

But I am okay.
Right now.

A Chemo Christmas

(With apologies to poet Clement Clarke Moore)

'Twas the night before Wellness and all through the house,
Not an Oncologist was stirring, nor even a spouse.
The stockings were hung by the chimney with care
In hopes that St. Nicholas would fill them with hair.

Inge's kids were all nestled, all snug in their beds
While visions of Wellness danced in their heads.
And she in her kerchief and I in my wig
Had just settled down for a long Wellness gig.

When out in the parking lot, there arose such a clatter
I sprang from my chair to see what was the matter.
And what to my wondering eyes should appear?
But a miniature sleigh and 8 tiny reindeer.

"On Taxol, On Compazine, Tamoxifen and more.
On Surgery, Radiation, Clean Lymph Nodes galore.
Now Dasher, now Dancer, now Prancer and Vixen,
Please work your healing and come in to fix 'em.

As I drew in my head and was turning around
Out of the elevator came St. Nick with a bound.
A bundle of cures he had flung on his back
And he smiled with red cheeks as he opened his pack.

Massage and nutrition all tied up in bows
T'ai Chi and Yoga 'til the immune system glows.
He left trumpets and flutes and even percussion
Along with fresh dreams, just ripe for discussion.

Then laying his finger aside of his nose
He presses the button: up the elevator he goes!
But I heard him exclaim ere he drove out of sight.
"Wellness to all and to all a good night."

The Door Closed

The door closed.

Silence ricocheted against windows
Bounced back toward the couch
And settled in the chair
That had been Renee's.

The door closed.

A chorus of "Good Luck!"
"We'll be thinking about you."
"You'll be in our prayers."
Rammed up against wood and hinges:
And abruptly stopped.

The door closed.

Eyes moved—some inward,
Some distracted, some frantically trying
To make contact with others in the group—
As the minutes ticked by slowly,
Weighted by the closed door.

"It was good that she came," said Inge.

The door closed.

(Note: The closing of the door indicates that support group is in session. Renee left group early that day for a stem cell transplant. She died during treatment.)

February Group

Sun arrows pierce through gray windows
Like heat-seeking missiles
Blasting open old scars and exposing buried hurts.

Some of us sit carefully
Dodging the light,
Listening to the vulnerable ones
Whose fears, tears, anguish and hope
Tumble out in halting narratives.

Feeling fragile
I try not to be moved.
But the resonance of their fears is too strong.

In Marge's tears for betrayed friendships and betrayed body,
I cry.
In Sue's angry tears for a broken relationship,
I cry.
In Connie's fears for a recurrence,
I cry.

The morning opened up
All of those places I didn't want to visit:
The geography of pain.

When the journey was over
We silently stood in a circle
Hand holding hand
Hand holding hand
Until our love, pain, hope, fear and strength
Traveled round and round
And we became one.

I glanced out the window.
There were no clouds on the horizon.

Message

The phone rang.
Renee died.
I picked up the headset.
Renee died.
Hello Jan, said Helen.
Renee died.

I looked out the window.
Renee died.
The red maple swayed in the breeze.
Renee died.
Goldfinches clustered around the feeder.
Renee died.
Hyacinths were opening their buds.
Renee died.

Thank you for calling, Helen.
Renee died.
I put down the phone.
Renee died.
I glanced at my calendar.
Renee died.
Chemo tomorrow.
Renee died.

Renee died.

Once

It used to be easy
To capture the spirit of this group:
The elation at Andy's graduation
Or Carol's joyous return to work.
Or the sudden sadness as
Renee shocked us with her burst of spirit—
Then sudden plummet—into death.

Before long, the fabric of the group I knew began unraveling.
New faces replaced the old before I was ready.
Sue's graduation and move, though I knew it was coming,
Was a personal loss.
I tried to catch her in a poem
But she slipped through the words.

Annette's elation at her freedom from cancer
Made me want to sing.
Her smile and vitality were electrifying!
She was like Rocky, on the big screen,
Running up those steps in Philadelphia,
Hands over head,
Music pounding,
Shouting of victory.

I was gone for two weeks.

When I returned, all images of Rocky had fled.
Annette was sitting in Renee's chair
Her courage intact,
Her spirit deflated.
"Another trial, Lord.
Another trial."

Last week I was sitting in Renee's chair.
I could not catch that in a poem,
Nor Sally's radiation burns,
Nor Marge's operation,
Nor Susan's pancreas.

Once upon a time,
I was a poet.
Once.

Mary's Story

Several years ago Mary joined our Wellness Community support group. A vibrant young woman, she had been diagnosed with brain cancer with a daunting prognosis of 6 months to live. Enduring surgery, radiation, and countless rounds of chemotherapy, she was determined to beat the odds.

Every three months she would report her test results to us. The day finally arrived when Mary rushed into group, waving her latest MRIs. "I'm so happy," she announced triumphantly. "There's nothing in my brain!"

They Want...

They want a poem.
Inge leans expectantly,
Wondering whether I have tapped the spirit
Of the group,
Framed it neatly
In measured lines
To ritually end the session.

They want a poem.
They want to know that there are beginnings
And endings to things—
Not the interminable waiting of cancer
Where tests are never conclusive
And even years can't shield against recurrence.

They want a poem
Because each of them has a story,
A wonderful, beautiful, terrifying story
Which shouts to a world
That doesn't take the time to listen.

They want a poem
Because in the midst of chaos,
Crisis and doubt,
A poem distills experience into basic truths.

They want a poem:
For poem is prayer.

REFLECTIONS

Creating healing partnerships

In life-threatening illnesses, the doctor-patient relationship plays a powerful role in the treatment and healing process, and yet most people spend more time choosing a car than a doctor. As these poems illustrate, different people need different things from their medical caregivers. If you feel secure knowing all you can about your illness, for example, you probably don't want the strong silent type as your doctor. If you want to fight aggressively with new clinical trials, you'll thrive with a doctor on the cutting edge in treatment. When a doctor's values and personality reflect some of your needs and values, you create a healing relationship. In medical care, one size does not fit all.

In 15 years I've gone through peaks and valleys with several oncologists. My first oncologist was excellent and I stayed with him until he moved. I chose a woman oncologist the second time, but discovered gender doesn't ensure empathy. Our styles clashed—and when my cancer returned, I needed someone I could totally trust. I found that in Dr. Julie Wiehl, whose kindness, patience, clinical skills and caring were superb. If I read about a new treatment, she already knew all about it. Plus she liked poetry—an excellent match for a poet patient like me.

When Dr. Wiehl left on sabbatical, I panicked. How would I find someone as well-suited to my temperament? Friends made suggestions and I "auditioned" oncologists as you'll see in "Wanted." That time was well spent and I was infinitely lucky to find Dr. Susan Luedke, who keeps my body and spirit alive with creative chemo, super clinical skills, a great sense of humor, and a lot of love. That sense of comfort and trust with my doctor and her caring staff makes my illness bearable.

Psychologists tell us that when people experience life-threatening situations, they often regress to the emotions of very young children. The doctor, nurse, or major caregiver can assume almost a parental role at times to the scared child in the adult patient. I found this true for me.

View from the Chemo Chair

What I could see from where I stood,
Were three chemo nurses up to no good.
Mixing their potions with devilish glee,
They turned toward the chairs looking for me.

Carrying needles of every size,
They hoped to catch my veins by surprise.
But even with all of their cleverest tricks,
My veins rolled away, needing two sticks.

Next came those hours trapped in the chair
With a blood pressure here and a catheter there.
And whenever they said not to move my IV,
My body invariably needed to pee.

I chatted with the others, snug in their chairs,
Some reading books; others saying prayers.
We shared all our secrets to stop side effects:
Like soy and shark cartilage with broccoli flecks.

As I glanced at the patients, curled up in their chairs,
I wondered what protocols they each called theirs.

The Decadron patients were easy to place—
Constantly moving like aliens in space.
At 3 in the morning, the whole house they clean,
And by 4, not a speck of dust can be seen.

The Neupogen patients were much more laid back.
With pillows and blankets, they'd rest and they'd snack.
Myself, I enjoyed a good shot of Procrit!
To give me the energy to run and stay fit.

The final "beep" came, like a school recess bell,
Calling our nurses to bandage us well.
Triumphant, we rose filled with fluids galore,
Shouting "Just one more treatment!" we dashed out the door.

To Our Nurses

They know us first by touch:
>   Circling the blood pressure cuff around an arm
>   Strumming their fingers to find a pulse
>   Stroking our skin for the perfect place for an IV.
They learn the geography of our veins better than we do.

And then, when chemo months sometimes turn into years,
Their touch deepens:

>   High fives when our counts are up
>   Huge hugs when we're feeling down
>   Generous smiles when we need them most.

Slowly the line between nurse and friend blurs.
Their touch travels now
Deep in the rivers of our souls.

Caregiving

I once had an oncologist who went on maternity leave. Of course, during that time I discovered a new lump at the edge of my breast and was in unparalleled panic. I called the office to see if one of the doctors could fit me in that week. The receptionist called back and said to come in at 11. I was so shaken I don't even remember driving to the medical building, much less where I parked.

Once in the waiting room, I felt faint with fear. Suddenly I heard a baby cooing. My oncologist stood there smiling, cradling her month-old baby, inviting me to hold her child as we walked into the examining room. She had come in from maternity leave just to see me, gave me the added pleasure of holding her baby, and then examined me. I've never felt more grateful for a single act of human love and kindness than I did that day. If angels exist, I know I have met one.

Dr. Luedke's Used Car and Body Shop

Sometimes I feel like an ancient used car
Marked with dents and dings—like my biopsy scar.
My paint is all peeling; my battery is low,
So she charges me with Procrit for get-up-and-go.

My engine required a complete overhaul:
For that she used gallons of Super Taxol.
Instead of just doing an oil and a lube,
She poured in the drugs through a thick IV tube.

When I desperately needed a powerful start
She opened a port right into my heart.
She revved up my engine with a powerful roar
Peeling strips of rubber with four on the floor.

Sometimes my shift gets stuck in first gear.
She helps me to cope by lending an ear.
And when my tires become worn and flat
She inflates them with Decadron, making them fat.

At times I feel weary and sad in my heart,
But a visit to her makes my outlook jump-start.
She's got jumper cables and great expertise,
Let Luedke's mechanics work on your disease.

So rev up your engines, push four to the floor—
With Luedke's great service, your spirits will soar.

Abandoned

When I was five,
I was scared when my parents went away on vacation.
They would be gone forever.

What if I broke my arm?
Or had a terrible nightmare? Or got sick?
Only my mother could cook chicken soup
And slice grilled cheese sandwiches
Just the way I like them.

When my parents returned,
I would not kiss them for days.

Now I'm an adult.
At 57, I have traveled the world on business
And am older than my oncologist.
And yet when she goes on vacation,
I become 5 again.

My stomach aches.
Dreams disturb my sleep.
I am alone again.
It feels like forever.

When Dr. Mommy returns,
My world becomes brighter, happier, safer.
But I still won't give her a hug.

Chameleon

When the doctor enters my examining room,
She never knows what she will find.

Sometimes I'm an enraged tiger, sapphire eyes blazing, pacing and
ready to pounce:
    Why didn't you tell me radiation would hurt so much?
    And look! I'm losing my hair! You said I wouldn't.

Other times I'm a stately ostrich, cloaked in well-groomed white
feathers, burrowing my head deep into the sand:
    No, I prefer not to look at my x-rays and test results.
    That is your domain. Just give me your recommendations, please.

Once I was a platypus, the oddest looking mammal on the planet:
    Patches of hair dotted my scraggy bald head
    One arm was much bigger than another, swelling with lympedema
    Radiation burns scarred my back and hips.
    Will you still treat me as human?

And sometimes I'm a cuddly panda, eager to please and be hugged:
    Oh, Doctor. That drug you prescribed completely stopped the
    nausea. I'm so lucky to have you as my oncologist.

I wait for my doctor to enter my world.
She should look at me first, not at my chart.
After all, who knows what she might find waiting in this room?

Wanted:
Superlative Oncologist

With excellent clinical skills
A soothing bedside manner
Tolerance for histrionic crying or sudden panic
And a charming sense of humor.
Being able to read the patient's mind would be a plus

That's the job description I had in mind when I went out to "audition" doctors to choose a new oncologist. My current oncologist, whom I loved, set the bar extremely high. When she left practice for a two-year sabbatical, I was bereft. I had already experienced the importance of a solid healing partnership with my oncologist, so I knew I had to put in the time upfront to find another.

Candidate number one was an older doctor with an excellent reputation—a kindly Dr. Marcus Welby, M.D. type. While not a real talker, he was a good listener until I burst into tears and he frantically looked for an escape hatch. But that was okay. His clinical exam seemed fine, until he finished prematurely. "Since I have breast cancer, shouldn't you check my breasts?" I asked. His face reddened at the crucial omission. I checked his name off of the list.

Candidate number two was in a convenient location and highly recommended by a patient I knew. This oncologist was very bright and very verbal. She did a thorough clinical exam and then we talked in her office. "What are you doing for bone pain?" she asked. "Nothing. I'm extremely lucky and haven't had any." She stared at me for a moment and then said, "I think you're in denial." My feathers ruffled at her response. Why did she presume to think she knew what I was feeling? And if no pain were a form of denial, I should be bottling and selling it to other cancer patients. This was followed by a discussion of treatment possibilities. I objected to one treatment since I had seen extreme nausea as a prominent side effect. "Oh, we have drugs now to control the nausea," she said. And yet her patient that I knew suffered one or two days each month with debilitating nausea.

We were clearly not communicating well, so I scratched her name off of the list.

Unfortunately I didn't have a third name and began to panic. A good friend in oncology said, "I know just the doctor for you. I'll call and get you an appointment right away." The appointment was on Halloween day, and my first introduction to the staff was in costume. Nurse Charlie, who took my history, was a clown, and Dr. Luedke swooped into the room as a witch. Was this an omen? As we talked, I liked her sense of humor and her knowledge of the most recent cancer treatments. When I asked what activities I should refrain from due to bone metastasis, she said, "Bungee jumping and parachuting for starters." I began to relax.

When Dr. Luedke did the clinical examination, I noted her concentration and intensity. Her fingers were intuitive and magical—like someone who divines for water. When she finished, she said. "The left lobe of your liver feels a bit hard and enlarged. I think we should do a CT scan to see what's going on." I almost fell off the examining table. This doctor had never met me, did not know my body, and yet was suggesting a scan. Afraid to ignore her findings, I decided to have the scan but told her I didn't deal well with waiting. It was late Friday afternoon. She said, "I'll see if we can schedule you for Saturday morning and I'll call as soon as they have the results." And she did.

My cancer had metastasized to my liver as she predicted, and we spent a long time talking about treatments. She asked my husband and me to come in on Monday morning, knowing we would have many questions and fears which could be resolved in that appointment. We knew instantly we had found the oncologist we sought—knowledgeable, personable, open, and caring.

Afterwards I pondered. I had seen two respected oncologists the week before Dr. Luedke and they had missed my liver metastasis. Someone was looking after me by sending me to Dr. Luedke. She literally saved my life, and continues to save my life through innovative, individualized treatment. She once said, "I consider my patients my friends." And that makes all the difference.

Small Craft Warnings

Singing in the shower and sudsing away,
My hand glides over my breast—
My heart stops.
I feel a lump.

A wave of nausea washes over me.
I can barely stand.
No! It can't be. Not cancer again.

I raise my hand and nervously circle my breast
Is there a new lump?
Or am I just imagining it?

My mind spins in futile circles,
My hands useless to detect what's really there.
I stand alone trying to quell my rising panic,
My tears mixing with the water in the shower.

Experience tells me to call my doctor
Not to drive myself crazy with worry.
Fear and pride face off
As I shiver and wrap myself in a towel.

My doctor is on leave.
I call the doctor's office to see whether
Anyone can fit me in.
Patty promises to call back in 20 minutes.

Fear animates me. I need to keep moving—
Circling around the house, noisily emptying the dishwasher,
Frantically picking up clothes and slamming doors shut.

My cat gives me a curious look,
Then moves out of the path of the tornado.

The phone rings.

My hand shakes as I pick up the receiver.
"Can you come in at noon today? Your doctor will see you."

I swoon with relief.
My cries for help have been heard.
Warmth surges though me
As I navigate these choppy waters.

I enter the examining room.

Very methodically my doctor checks every inch
In the breast area,
Moving her fingers forward and back,
Forward and back.
Once her fingers stopped—and I could barely breathe.
She slowly retraced her fingers over a quadrant.
Finally she was satisfied.

"You're feeling the end of a rib," she concluded.
"A rib?" I sputtered.
She guided my hand so I could recognize that lump.

As my fear subsided,
I marveled at the enormous gift she had given me.
My confidence in her caregiving was so powerful,
I knew I would survive.

"The end of a rib," I grinned,
"Just the end of a rib."

The Butterfly Brigade
In the Susan G. Komen Race for the Cure

Early one morn on a hot, muggy day
Thousands of racers wended their way
Toward an arch of balloons glowing pink in the sun:
The Race for the Cure had finally begun.

With a sleek, running style bounding out of the gate,
Doctor Dee Garcia led the competitive slate.
When the finish line loomed, she gave a great thrust—
But a 70 year-old left poor Dee in the dust.

Julie captained our strong 5K team
Weaving a path through the vast human stream.
With butterfly logos on heads, backs, or butts,
Our blue-shirted group drove the other teams nuts!

Donna and Heather set a very fast pace
With Jo, Pam and Sharon vying for space.
When we saw the big sign that proclaimed the first mile
Our team settled in with some sweat and a smile.

When Toni and Linda jogged by Mile Two,
The asphalt and concrete were baking our crew.
With feet growing weary and brows getting hot,
We foraged for shade while we kept up our trot.

With the Mississippi on our left and the Arch to our right,
We could see the 1K: an awesome pink sight.
Thousands of Survivors wheeled, walked or ran
With a triumphant spirit—the ultimate "I can!"

Somebody has to bring up the rear.
Two Rachels and Susan did so with cheer,
Pregnant with Braeden, who enjoyed his first race,
Kicking poor Susan to keep up the pace.

When the finish line finally came into view,
There were roses and hugs—and a race to the loo.
At the end we were sweaty and tired—but sure:
Each year we'll keep running until there's a cure.

The Butterfly Brigade of staff and patients proudly represents
the St. Louis Cancer And Breast Institute (2002).

CLOSE-UPS

Examining family ties

Cancer and other life-threatening illnesses magnify and intensify our closest relationships to parents, children, spouses, lovers, relatives, and friends. These bonds can be a source of strength or complication. Marriages become closer, for example, or partners decide to divorce.

I've chosen to focus on the strength I derived from the maternal relationship: from my adventurous grandmother who emigrated from Hungary to the United States through Ellis Island in 1914; from my mother, who came from California to St. Louis to take care of me during my first round of cancer; and from my daughter, whose life and security have been affected by my illness. Out of the strain of serious illness come moments of anger and doubt, but also moments of exquisite kindness and love.

Ellis Island

Songs from Ellis Island simmer in my soul
Strong portents from the past
Churning myths and memory
Myths and memory
Into a simple soup:
My past.

The photos in the island museum loom large:
Peasant women in hand-woven cloth
Some holding baskets,
Others holding children,
Staring straight at the camera:
Solemn, defiant, self-contained.

"Have you ever seen so many babushkas in one room?"
Laughs another visitor,
Enchanted as I am by the relics around us.
We wander carelessly through the centuries
Seeking likenesses, remembrances, tokens of our past.

*My Grandmother Sophia Kun Arvai
with daughter Zsuzsanna in 1914*

The next exhibit makes me gasp:
In a glass-enclosed table lie 5 tiny pairs of shoes.
From Greece, some baby slippers with colored beads and
dainty toes;
From Russia, some leather-laced boots, stiff with mud and age;
But in the center
The gentlest white leather, molded so delicately
For the softest of baby feet.

You could reach through the centuries
And almost touch the baby toes
And hear the soothing lullabies
Crooned by women with hard, peasant faces.

In the silent halls of Ellis Island
Where the past whispers in every language
And shouts of hardship and sometimes despair:
A peasant's eyes look right at mine
And the softness of those baby shoes
Cradles my soul.

My Mother Helen Arvai Stack with daughter Janice in 1945

Thereness

I had a mastectomy and 16 lymph nodes removed in 1987, the standard treatment at that time. My mother flew in from California to take care of me. When I opened my eyes after surgery, drugged and groggy, she was there, sitting next to my bed, knitting quietly and ready to do anything I asked. That day my mind drifted in and out of consciousness, through a confusing jumble of past, present and future, but each time I opened my eyes, there was my mother—solid, caring, comforting. I'll never forget the steadfastness of her love, her thereness, her being a mother again to her 42 year-old daughter.

Ballet

When I was first diagnosed with
cancer, a shy wisp of a girl would hide
behind my knees when strangers
came. I was more terrified of leaving
Julie at this vulnerable age than I was
of death itself. When I took her to
ballet lessons, I'd sit on the side of the
gym and tears would flow as I
watched her dance—beautiful,
innocent, completely caught up in the
music and movement. These moments
were some of the most beautiful in my
life. I vowed to do whatever it took to
stay alive until Julie was at least 12
and could survive without a mother.

My Daughter Julie Newhouse with cat Toby in 1985

When a Parent Has Cancer:
A Teenager's View

(Note: When my cancer metastasized in 1997, my daughter did not like to talk or think abut it, but she wrote about her feelings in a school assignment about "an event that changed my life." Julie calls herself "the girl" in her essay.)

BY JULIE NEWHOUSE

The sound of the incessant ticking of the right turn signal echoes in the ear of the girl. Her useless left foot taps impatiently while waiting for the signal to turn green. She drives quickly, eyes scanning the parking lot for an empty spot. Parking in the shade of a small tree, she strides confidently towards the ominous building. To her left, ambulances come and go rapidly. To her right lies a vacant helicopter pad, and directly in front of her, the revolving doors.

This girl, in particular, carries a small plant with fresh pink flowers in one hand and a backpack full of heavy books in the other. She pushes through the glass as if she knows what to expect, as if she knows where to go, how to act, or how to feel. But, in truth, behind the collected and mature façade, she is scared and alone.

The halls inside the building are long and cold. The light comes from drab ceiling lights, stationed mechanically every ten feet or so. Her footsteps echo on the cold tile floor. Her walk, once confident and purposeful, becomes timid and uncertain. As she approaches the last door at the end of the hall, her heart feels heavy and full of dread. Nurses brush past her in a flurry of activity as if she does not exist. One of the mechanical nurses walks into the room, her destination, carrying more ice chips for room 323. The person in 323 is no longer her mother, but a meaningless number. "323, 323" echoes in the girl's brain as she enters the room.

The woman in the bed is a stranger. She is not the woman who has provided and given strength to the girl. This woman is pale. Instead of exuding life, life is being pumped into her through breathing tubes and IVs. This woman does not seem strong and confident. She seems scared and alone. The woman in the hospital bed can't be her mother. This woman is receiving care and needing strength. Her mother has always been the one to give her strength. If only she and her mother could share in their common loneliness and fear.

With trembling hands, the girl places the flowering plant on the night stand and kisses her mother's forehead. The doctor breezes in, spitting out high tech medical terms that drift out the window into the warmth of the afternoon. "Cancer." That word sticks. It hops into the girl's mind and runs around in circles. It has a hollow, dead sound to it, but it sticks, lodging itself deep within her heart.

She feels an irresistible urge to run away rising up in her chest. If only she could run back through those doors and drive. Drive until all of her family's pain is left behind. But the girl standing next to her mother is not a child anymore. She is seventeen. She has been gaining strength and courage for all seventeen of those years. Her mother has taught her to be strong. But now she must be strong for her mother.

If she were still the blue-eyed, blonde-haired little girl, maybe her ears would not have heard the harsh truths. Perhaps the gray-haired doctor would have left out the grim survival statistics. Gazing into her mother's face, she looks beyond the tubes and hospital gown. Deep within her mother's eyes, the strength and love she has always possessed and shared with her child still prevails. And with each passing day, the strength of both mother and daughter grows, not falling victim to cancer.

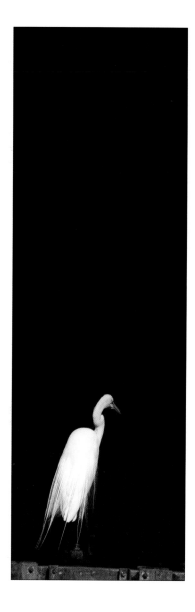

Without you
There is no resonance
No ripples on the pond
When pebbles hit the water.

Just a silent sinking.

Guilt:
A Mother/Daughter Duet

When my daughter was in the midst of making college decisions, my cancer returned, ten years after the original diagnosis. We had planned to visit three prospective colleges that summer. But when Julie gave me her list, I was astonished. "I thought you wanted to go to Boston. These colleges are all less than four hours from home." "Doesn't that tell you something, Mom?" I groaned under the weight of guilt. In what I now recognize as denial, I thought I could shield my daughter and her dreams from my illness. Luckily my cancer responded to new drugs and by Julie's senior year, we began to trust that I would live. So off we went to explore Boston, which won her heart. Julie enrolled in Boston University that fall.

Near the end of her first semester, my cancer returned, this time in the liver—a terrifying prospect. That spring Julie wrote a long letter telling us she was transferring to St. Louis University for her sophomore year:

"...Being away made me appreciate and realize the closeness we have. Mom, I know you want me to do what's best for me and choose whatever college I want, regardless of its distance from home. But I don't think I could live with myself if I spent what could be the last times we have together thousands of miles away. I have my entire life ahead of me to live and go wherever I want... I don't want to look back and regret not spending the time we still have together..."

Julie's letter was incredibly moving, but guilt still nibbled at my heart, knowing she was giving up Boston because of my illness. My oncologist provided the needed perspective. "Trust your daughter. Julie knows what she feels and where she needs to be." Her words freed me from the shackles of guilt and enabled me to embrace Julie's adult decision. Each weekend when she stops off at home to do her laundry and eat a home-cooked meal, we go for a long walk and talk together. I realize anew how deeply I love her and how happy I am she chose to live close to home.

When Julie was 6, I prayed to live until she was 12 and more independent. When Julie was 12, I prayed I would get to see her graduate from high school. On May 16, 2003, Paul and I watched Julie graduate from St. Louis University. I revel in the fact that each year has been a gift.

Sea Change

Following the wave-etched line of pebble and shells
I walk down the windswept beach
As I have done so many times this trip,
Trying to grasp the elusive truth
Dancing between the waves.

I see my daughter then
Far out in the lake, head bobbing brightly in the waves,
Swimming with strokes strong and pure
Sun glinting on tan arms.

"You're out too far!" I shout.
The wind wisps the words back in my face.
"You're out too far."

Years ago on this beach
She held my hand,
Both of us jumping and squealing
As waves lapped our legs
And drenched our clothes.

Now she is sixteen
Alone in the sea
Swimming beyond the reach of my hand.
The reach of my voice.

In the shimmering waves
I watch her swim—
Powerful strokes, playful strokes—
Farther out than I have ever dared to go.
A fierce pride washes over me:
She is my daughter.

I pull back.
The water laps against my ankles as the sun slowly sets.

Lake Michigan: 1996

Now

When I was first diagnosed with cancer, I was terrified I would die and abandon my young daughter when she needed me the most. When I saw other mothers with older daughters going shopping or out to lunch, I cried because Julie and I wouldn't have that future.

Last month when Julie and I were having lunch at an Italian restaurant, a waiter tripped, flipping a pizza off of its plate and onto the floor. We tried hard not to laugh, but each time we swallowed our laughter, one look from the other would start us giggling again.

Suddenly I realized that even though my cancer had spread over the years, through the stabilizing power of Taxotere and Herceptin, I had been given the opportunity to do what I wanted most. To other diners, we looked like any other mother and daughter having lunch together. But to me it was the deepest pleasure: a pure enjoyment of living in the moment with a daughter who had grown up happy and self-assured.

The Lake

Almost every summer
A poem is born:
Midwived by beach and sun and sea
And baptized in stunning Michigan sunsets.

The brilliant reds, oranges and purples
Wash away my tattered layers of self.

No more the mother, the wife, the friend.
Here life is distilled to its essence.

I become the gull gliding toward shore
The sailboat dancing wild with the wind
Pebbles tossed and polished by waves
That curl and unfurl toward the shore.

I am the child being teased by the waves
The eager girl trying hard to skip stones
The teenager made bashful by boys
The camper entranced by the fire.

I am the old couple, too, slowly climbing the dune,
Shoulders almost touching,
Watching the sun splash reds and pinks
Across the sky, then slowly melt into dark.

No longer does my child, my girl, or my teen
Walk with me on the familiar trail.

Perhaps one summer she will return—
Giving birth to her own special poem.

PERSPECTIVES
Exploring new experiences

The lens of cancer at some level colors everything you see and feel, revealing multiple ways to explore and understand your illness and providing external contexts and events that help you redefine yourself in the larger world. Given the uncertainty of cancer, I made a conscious decision to say "Yes!" to any appealing opportunities while I still could walk, talk, work, love, and play. When I die, I want to be draped in a quilt of splendid memories, not wrapped in a tattered cloak of regrets.

So, one month after major chemotherapy ended in 2000 (the big guns of Adriamycin and Taxol followed by Xeloda), I was on a plane, my professional wig tucked in place, to work in London for a week and then to vacation in Paris for two days. Paris was so liberating, I immediately took off my wig and called my fuzzy head *Paris chic*. My consulting work took me to Boston, New York and other places, where I stayed an extra day to take in those vibrant cities. My husband and I cashed in a CD for a dream vacation in the Caribbean.

Each place, each experience was saying "Yes!" to life, even on days that were painful. And each experience provided new ways to view my illness and come to terms with it. These poems reflect the rich mosaic of those days and the diverse ways of seeing and coping with a life-threatening illness.

Bald

I stare in the mirror
Slowly stroking my bald head.

A ladybug lands on my head,
Her red and black wings shining like a jewel in the desert.

For the first time in days,
I smile.

Masquerade

By day I masquerade as a professional,
Every hair in place, expensive briefcase at my side.

But as night falls, so does my charade.
Deftly I peel off my wig,
Freeing my bald head to cool with relief.
Then I carefully strip off my eyebrows.
Finally I take off my prosthesis,
That false breast that allows others to forget I have cancer.

I ease into my soothing fleece warm-up suit,
Settle deep into the pillows of my favorite chair,
And sigh—sometimes with pleasure,
Sometimes with exhaustion—
But always with relief from playing a role
I never auditioned for.

I watch the embers glow and fade in the fireplace
And send my soul into deepest relaxation.
When tomorrow dawns,
My costume is ready.
The show goes on.

The Flip Side of Cancer

Do you see the IV bag as half-full or half-empty? Even cancer has some virtues...

That hard lump in your breast turns out to be fat. It's the first time in your life that your fat makes you happy!

The mammography machine squeezes your breast like a pancake. You swear you'll never eat at IHOP again.

After your first chemo treatment, you decide to invest in Zofran, Compazine, and Kytril. You know you'll help them produce dividends!

You're finally bald. It's impossible to have a bad hair day.

When the med tech brings you the results of your CBCs, you wonder whether you'll ever earn "A"s again.

You're overjoyed with your clean bone scan. The only "hot spots" are in Baghdad.

The radiation technologist draws lines all over your body. You no longer enjoy paintings by Paul Klee.

You love your new diet: soy, seaweed and shark cartilage pizza followed by Krispy Kreme doughnuts. After all, the nutritionist said to balance your diet.

Your kid wins the Regional Spelling Bee as the only child who can spell "Adriamycin." See. That drug was good for something.

The High Wire

When I was little,
I learned to run before I walked;
To jump before I climbed.
I was an amazing dynamo of movement.
On stormy days,
I would race with the wind
Trying to beat it around my house.

After I grew up and needed chemo,
My adult self would sit in the recliner
Tethered to the IV.
But my imagination would go to the circus—
Balancing and dancing on the high wire—
Performing death defying flips,
Encouraged by the crowd below.

Finally came the triumphant day:
The end of chemo!
No more weekly doctor's check-ups.
No more hovering nurses and IVs.
No more weekly blood tests.
I danced out of that chemo room like a liberated child.

So why, weeks later, do I feel so down?
Where is that skip in my step?
That joy in my soul?
I send my imagination back to the high wire
But my steps now are tentative
My balance shaky.

Suddenly I look down.
The net is gone.
No doctors. No chemo. No weapons against cancer.
I stand alone on the high wire
Wondering whether I have the courage
To take the next step.

Thanksgiving

When I die,
I'd like to be buried on a lazy autumn afternoon
With the yawning sun basting the leaves
In deep reds, browns, and yellows.

When the earth smells damp and rich,
And birds and squirrels clatter about,
Preparing for winter.

A languid laziness soothes my limbs
And blankets me in warmth
As I stretch contented in the autumn sun.

Death has touched me gently
With his long frosted fingers,
Reminding me that one day he will return for good.

But, for now, I listen to the gentle drone of the bees,
Revel in the drift of swirling leaves,
And cherish the beauty of shadow and light.

Paris 2000

There is a time
Outside of time
An iridescent bubble shimmering
Before its brilliance bursts.

And so it is
On vacation with cancer.
A time to live in the moment:
Feeling the cobbled streets of Paris under your feet
And the heat simmering and rising in the Place de Notre Dame
And smelling sweet cappuccino, steaming under colored umbrellas
Dotting the sidewalk cafes like festive circus balloons.

And you walk and you walk
Watching the endless human stream:
Lovers languidly strolling on the banks of the Seine.
Old women, hunched over canes,
Mouths moving silently, drawn to the spired Cathedral.
Young people, flagged in brilliant colors and fueled by rollerblades,
Slicing swiftly through the crowd with the careless ease of youth.
And there, on a bench under a tree, rests a young woman
Quietly nursing her baby,
Oblivious to the human carnival swirling around her.

And you breathe this all in.
And you shudder with joy.

So you shoulder your luggage and heave it into a locker,
Shoving the heaviest bag,
Weighted with CAT scans, tumor markers, and terror,
Into the cold metallic bin.
You listen to the clatter of the coins as you lock the door
And—without a backward glance—
Stride confidently into the streets.

Your bag will be there when you return.

Transaction

Two weeks after surgery
I went to the bank to make a withdrawal.
The teller, an older woman with a comfortable smile,
Often gave lollipops to my daughter.

I pushed the withdrawal slip across the counter.
The teller smiled.
"I have breast cancer," I blurted out.
I didn't even know her name.
"I have breast cancer," I cried.

She put her hand over mine.
"I'm so sorry."
We stood as still as a tableau,
Her kindness flowing into me.

Then the real world returned,
As people lined up behind me.
The teller gave me my money,
And completed our transaction.

September 11: Another View

I have been living too long with terror:
Minute cancerous cells, like stealth missiles,
Hover in my body,
Ready to attack my bones—
Imploding their strength, reducing them to rubble.
And then those cells stalk again,
Cautiously creeping
From their cavernous lairs,
This time searching for my brain, my liver, my lungs.

I have hugged my chemo friends
When they've been told
There are no new chemicals left in the arsenal.
No more secret weapons to defeat their cancers.
And I have seen the terror etched on the faces of family and friends
When they face the unthinkable:
The death of their mother, father, child, or friend.

I have lived with terrorists in my body for four years,
Learning not to cry,
But to cling desperately to life and hope.
Some day my tears will flow freely—
Joining those of our nation in a cleansing flood.
But today, I am lucky.
I only have cancer.

Moon Dance

Paul and I chose to celebrate the end of my seemingly endless chemotherapy by visiting Persie, an older friend, in the British Virgin Islands. This visit was going to be different from others, because I was emotionally and physically depleted from my chemo, and we heard that Persie's Alzheimers was getting worse. We didn't know what to expect.

The evening we arrived, the sky was cloudy and dark. We were happy Persie remembered who we were, although she forgot other things, like the day of the week or where she kept her house keys. The three of us strolled down to the mile-long, sugar-sand beach, speckled with stately palm trees and warmed by the Caribbean breezes. As we walked, the moon edged out from behind a cloud, lighting the tips of the foaming waves and Persie's fine gray hair, and highlighting bits of green phosphorescence in the sea. Almost simultaneously, a steel drum band started to play at a nearby resort.

Persie loved to dance. So we kicked off our shoes and started dancing in the sand—alone, all together, in twos—it didn't matter. What mattered was how much we laughed as we tried to do fancy rock and roll spins and twists as well as the funky chicken, whipping sand in all directions. With the ocean playing bass and the moon like a strobe light, we danced our hearts out until we fell, laughing and gasping on the sand. We hadn't seen Persie so vibrant and happy in years. On that glorious evening, it didn't matter that Persie had Alzheimers and I had cancer.

When my soul needs nourishment, that magical evening under the full moon and glistening seas makes my heart dance.

Night Vision

Late at night after my visitors left
And the nurses were done doling out pills,
I would slip out of my hospital bed,
Grab a warm blanket,
And climb onto the cold marble windowsill.

Resting my head against the cold glass,
I'd snuggle the blanket around me
And survey the world from the 13th floor.

Cars and trucks raced down Kingshighway,
But the sound was muffled by the thick windows.
Looking up, I saw stars sprinkled above the city's glow—
Reminders of balmy Michigan nights at the beach.

I would start to tremble, then, and pull my blanket tighter,
Not wanting to leave until I saw the ice skaters
Whirling in the yellow glow of Forest Park.
My soul swirled and danced with the graceful couples,
Skating to music I could not hear.

Then the loneliness hit—like a sharp blow to my heart.
I sat suspended between earth and stars on that cold ledge,
Utterly alone with my cancer.

I vowed when I finished treatment
I would buy ice skates and join the skaters in the park.

Months later, I purchased skates for my family.
Out of practice, we were a motley group,
Sprawling, grabbing onto each other, giggling and silly,
Trying to look graceful while our ankles splayed and wobbled.

As the afternoon sun dipped low in the west,
I looked up toward the corner room on the 13th floor.
Executing a short, shaky spin, I beamed with a heroine's smile.

After all, someone up there might be watching.

Cancer Dreams

Sometimes the tentativeness of cancer drapes itself around me.
The weight of its cocoon slows down my steps
Muffles my words
And adds a ponderous weight to my thoughts,
My movements,
My soul.

I have grappled with my disease
Examined it from every angle
Trying to find some center in its amorphous shape.

The only constant is fluidity.
One day's prognosis, hopes and fears can change in a moment.
Feelings dance,
        flutter,
              tumble,
                    and crash.
Laugh uproariously,
      sob relentlessly,
            float on clouds,
                 freeze in flecks of ice,
                    banter, canter,
                       sing and sigh.

I want to emerge from this cancer cocoon:
To burst open its metastatic bonds
To believe once again in the sanctity of my body.

My wings want to burst forth
Opening their brilliance to greet the sun
And drift where the gentle breeze takes them.

Instead, my wings are bound tightly around me
Like old shoelaces, shabby and torn,
So knotted and tangled, they will never let me free.
When I dream, I dream of flight.

INNER LIGHT

Creating hope and healing

The cancer experience begins in darkness—in fear, isolation, doubt, and loss—and yet regardless of the prognosis, can be transforming. It can open your eyes to new ways of seeing and experiencing or close your eyes in rigid fear. It can drop you into the depths of despair, but also can show you ways to rise and transcend. No one wants Cancer as a teacher, but the lessons it teaches in patience, empathy and the richness of living in the moment are invaluable. As you look outside for help—from friends, family, church, support groups, medical staff, and books—you begin to build a solid foundation for understanding your illness and its progression. But the real source of hope and light comes from within: the values you possess and strengthen deep inside you.

Since I have metastatic cancer, a medical cure is not an option. But healing is. Healing involves accepting the cards you are dealt and playing the best game you can. For me, healing occurred as I learned to live in the moment, to sort out my values, and to appreciate the richness of each day. Healing occurs when I talk to newly diagnosed cancer patients and can allay some of their fears. And healing occurs in a new optimism inventing an attitude of *Stage 5: Staying Alive* and surrounding myself with other "terminal" patients who are committed to living life to the fullest. Healing also occurs in my poems, being able to transform my fears and experience into art.

For me, healing also means I wake up each morning in gratitude for an extra day of life. Some of those days are frightening and painful, but most are not. Knowing I have more days left is a gift I never expected from metastatic cancer. When you find and live in that inner light—whether you call it God or spirit or hope or soul—you transform your world and that of others around you.

Sometimes transformation comes:
A silent drift of snow and ice
Dusts the land:
Like a photographer's lens,
It mutes the trees in grays and whites
Capturing a world suspended in time.

Touch

Tenderness travels deep during cancer

Slowly stoking a fire of comfort and, sometimes, desire.

The softness of skin on skin as he slowly strokes my hand,

The gentle balm as he brushes my hair,

The massage of fragrant oils he rubs upon my feet

Ignite the warmth of glowing coals—

And, sometimes, the flame of desire.

There are many ways to warm the heart.

Charms

Some women collect charm bracelets.
I collect moments
Burnishing them until they radiate light.

Reflecting the glow of unexpected kindness,
They circle me with warmth.

My best friend Suellen showed up after surgery with a basket full
of colorfully wrapped gifts, one for each night I would be in the
hospital. She instructed me to let my daughter Julie choose and
open my gift each night. My husband Paul always managed to
sneak 6 year-old Julie past the nurse's station, since she needed to
see me each day to make sure I was all right. Once the basket
was there, however, Julie spent time feeling, shaking, and
choosing just which box to open. One night it was fancy
chocolates that we all shared; another night an issue of *The New
Yorker* that we skimmed for cartoons. And the last night—the
most wonderful, furry teddy bear. "Aren't you too old for teddy
bears, Mom?" Julie asked, cuddling the bear as she snuggled next
to me in the hospital bed. "You're never too old for teddy bears,"
I assured her. "Well, do you want me to take him home tonight
and make him a bed and stuff so he'll be ready when you come
home tomorrow?" "That sounds like a great plan." As Julie happily
skipped out, one hand holding Paul's and the other wrapped
around the bear, I marveled at the wisdom of Suellen's gifts.
Instead of Julie being apprehensive about coming to the hospital,
her curiosity and love for surprises made each night a holiday.

❖   ❖   ❖

The day I came home from the hospital, Paul announced he had
a surprise for me in the kitchen. We walked in, and instead of
seeing the shabby white kitchen table that came with the house,
there was a gleaming natural oak table of exquisite grain. I ran
my hand over the surface, feeling the warm smoothness of the
wood. "It's our old table," Paul said. "I took it apart, stripped it,

sanded it, and varnished it. What do you think?" I was speechless. Each night after his visit, Paul had taken his worry and fears for me and worked them out through the wood, transforming a shaky old table into an object of beauty. The kitchen is often the heart of a home, and seeing what Paul did with the table showed me again how solid we were as a family. We would survive.

❖   ❖   ❖

When my cancer returned, I was devastated. I stopped at the medical supply house to order a new prosthesis, and Dale, who has helped me for years, commented that I seemed pretty down. "My cancer's come back," I cried. "My cancer's come back." Dale was concerned and sympathetic as she wrapped my purchase. Shortly after I returned home, the doorbell rang. I opened the door, and a courier gave me a small box. Puzzled, I opened it. Inside was a beautiful terra cotta angel holding a pink ribbon. I was so overwhelmed by Dale's unexpected kindness that I glowed for the rest of the afternoon.

❖   ❖   ❖

On most Thursday mornings, no matter what I'm doing—working, consulting, reading, driving, gardening—a sense of warmth envelops me, and I stop to enjoy it. It comforts me that a book club in Virginia, *Bread for the Journey*, who has never met me, ends their weekly meeting with a prayer—and my name is in it. My good friend Sharon, who moved to Virginia and was a member, told the group about my cancer and my writing, and they adopted me. I can feel the power of their prayers cutting through the jumble of my daily life and offering me peace. To all my friends who pray for me daily, including all the Lannings, Stacks, and Newhouses as well as Mrs. Dwyer who attended a Miracle Mass in her nursing home each Tuesday for me, I am infinitely grateful.

The Scar

After my mastectomy, I saw nothing but bandage for days.
And then one morning the interns scrambled in with the resident
For the great unveiling of the scar.
I felt like I was on TV.
They slowly peeled back the bandages,
And six heads swiveled closer for a better view.

"Wow! Dr. Ballin did a great job! That's fine work!"
"Look at those tiny stitches. Awesome!"
I felt like an object at a fraternity party.
They chattered as if the scar were not part of a person.

When they left, I slowly peered down
Looking at the bright line of red x's where my breast used to be.
I felt curiously detached.
The whole process of biopsy, cancer and surgery
Occurred so fast, it wasn't real yet.
The scar and the missing breast were not yet me.

The nurses came in to rebandage me.
"Your doctor really did a fine job," they assured me.
"In a few years you won't even notice it."

When my husband came to take me home,
I told him the scar was not terrible.
"Let me know when you are ready to see it."
Several days passed, and he hadn't asked.

Finally I said, "I know you don't want to see the scar yet,
But I NEED you to see it. I need you to see it."
The air in the bedroom was still as I unbuttoned my blouse.
I looked away as he surveyed my chest.
"Hey. This is much better than I thought.
This is going to be all right," he said.

And it was.

Journey

Gently peel off the layers

       Your coat
       Your sweater
       Your blouse
       Your bra

Gaze in awe at your body

       Your breath flowing like a whisper
       Your heart lightly drumming its song
       Your ribs standing sentry in silence
       Your hands gently tracing your scar

Go deeper still
Swim in the sweet rivers of your soul

Miracle

Sometimes miracles happen, and one of the *Stage 5: Staying Alive Club* members is a literal example. Diagnosed with a Stage 4 terminal recurrence of leiomyo sarcoma in 2000, Wendy's disease was in an advanced state. None of the traditional chemotherapies or radiation treatments she tried could kill her rapidly growing cancer. Her last hope was a clinical trial based in Chicago to try Gleevac (the new wonder drug for leukemia). Wendy barely got into the trial—she filled the last space—and saw this as an omen that she belonged in this study. She commuted back and forth from St. Louis to Chicago for treatments and tests, certain that Gleevac would be her miracle. She was ecstatic!

Two months and many treatments later, the clinical trial doctor told Wendy he was dropping her from the study. Gleevac just wasn't working for her. "But you can't do this! Please let me stay," she pleaded. "I've tried everything else and nothing works! What am I supposed to do?" "There's nothing we can do. Go home and get your affairs in order. You probably have 3-6 months to live."

Wendy returned to St. Louis a defeated woman. The drugs had bloated her face almost beyond recognition and squeezed every ounce of energy out of her body. She sank into a deep depression, looking like death itself. But Dr. Luedke, her oncologist, never gave up. After detailed research, she started Wendy on a newly released pill, Temodar. Four months later, most of Wendy's tumors had shrunk or disappeared altogether. It was mid-December. Wendy was proclaimed the official Christmas miracle! A month later, the tumors in her lung shrank as well. Wendy literally catapulted from near-death back into her energetic, optimistic life.

It's been 13 months since that death sentence was issued in Chicago, with no appreciable growth of disease to be found on CT scans and x-rays. Will the cancer come back? No one knows. But right now Wendy, her husband, and 22 year old daughter are living each day to the fullest. Stage 5: Staying alive! It can happen.

Odds of Survival: 10 to 1

May you be the One!

Show Time

Gardening liberates my mind.
Humming an old *South Pacific* show tune,
I pulled weeds like *Nellie Forbush*—
"the cockeyed optimist!"—
Convinced those dandelions wouldn't spread
When I wasn't looking.

And the *Phantom of the Opera* guided me
As I sang my way through the honeysuckle
Yanking out the extra vines choking the clematis.
As my voice strained to hit the high note—
"The Phan...tom of the..." I stopped.

I realized I was joyfully singing out loud,
Something I hadn't done since starting chemo.
Among the many cancer losses
I never noticed *singing* on the casualty list—
Until the chemo stopped and the tunes returned.

Only four days were left before restarting chemo.
I ran to get the spade to plant more coreopsis,
Belting out *Bloody Mary* on the way.
My neighbor just stared at me.

So many songs. So few days.
My family and neighbors may suffer
"Now ain't that too damn bad!"

(TO KIRK)

So Fine

I'm so fine.
Lordy, I'm so fine.
Did you ever see a beak so sleek?
Or the fashion slash of my jet black streak?
Damn. I'm in style.
Those dull brown birds lust for my feathers
And choke with desire for my red-hot scarf.
But it's my sexy black beret that really gets them!
Trés, trés chic! And way cool.
Oh, those birds are so plain!
I'll deign to give them one last look.
Lordy!
I am *so* fine.

Autumn in Cambridge

Silently they come
Swiftly gliding through the water
Silver rowing shells
Ablaze in the sinking sun.

The sound of a splash startles me
As an oarsman missed his beat.
And the "Huh, Huh, Huh" of the coxswain
Bleats softly through the air.

I lie on the grassy bank:
A refuge between the silent river
And the muted growl of Cambridge traffic.

In front of me, a bee lands on clover
Clumsily climbs on top of the blossom
Until it arcs toward the ground.
Slowly he siphons the last sip of nectar.

Quietly I watch,
Suspended on my green island.

Aloft

Leslie had a particularly hard time during chemo and radiation, losing all of her hair and most of what she ate. So, she and her husband decided to celebrate the end of treatment with a trip to the Caribbean. Regaled in island garb with an exotic flower tucked in her wig, Leslie walked with Bill down the steps of the tiny prop plane. As they passed the propeller, its intense wind flipped the wig off of Leslie's head, sending it rolling like a piece of tumbleweed down the runway. Leslie screamed as she touched her fuzzy, bald head, while Bill took off after the elusive wig, gathering bits of dust and gravel in its tumbling path. Spectators from the plane watched as Bill made a valiant lunge, but came up empty as a gust of wind sent the wig aloft into the beautiful waves of the Caribbean.

At first shocked, and then laughing and crying simultaneously at Bill's heroic but fruitless effort, Leslie wasn't sure what to do. She tried to wrap her hands over her baldness. A passenger who witnessed the drama put her arm around Leslie and said, "You have a beautiful head. You don't need to hide it. Don't let anything ruin your lovely vacation." After the initial shock, Leslie and Bill accepted their loss with humor and grace and felt liberated as they walked, one hairy and one hairless, toward a much happier stage of their lives.

The Lone Palm Tree

You're laughing at me!
Don't think I can't hear you.
I can see the smirk on your face
As you stare at my balding branches and spindly arms.
Trees have to stretch, too.
I sure don't notice your human limbs holding still for 15 years!
And so my belly looks a little shaggy.
At least it's real.
None of that anorexic Barbie Doll look for me!

Bet you didn't know I had a modeling career once.
Where do you think that Dr. Seuss guy
Got the inspiration for all those grinches and loraxes?
Not from any ordinary maple or sweet gum, I can tell you that.
And just because I didn't make it into "Green Eggs and Ham"
Doesn't make me a loser.
You wouldn't want to be "in a box"
Or "with a fox" either.

So hold your sarcasm and snide remarks.
See me for what I really am:

A single tree
Battered by wind and storm
Who still raises her arms in joy each day
To greet the morning sun.

Legacy

Do not try to rescue the driftwood.
Let the sand scour its surface
And the waves wash it clean.

Wait for the storm to subside.
Listen to the gentling of the waves.
Finger the smoothness of the wood.
This is your legacy.

About the Author

JAN NEWHOUSE directs Jan Newhouse Associates, a communications consulting firm serving global companies. She has taught writing and English at the University of Missouri, Meramec Community College and currently teaches MBA students at Boston's Hult International Business School.

An active writer, Jan has published articles for professional and academic journals as well as feature articles for general audiences. Her poems have been published both locally and nationally. *Moon Dance* is her first book of poems.

A Phi Beta Kappa graduate of the University of Michigan, Jan earned her bachelors and masters degrees in English. She lives in St. Louis with her husband and daughter and has been inspired to write by the courage and stories of those she has met facing life-threatening illnesses.

Photo Credits

MARTY CLARKE is an avid photographer whose photographs have been shown in exhibits and purchased through local galleries. Marty is a physician assistant and doctoral student in clinical psychology, specializing in medical and psychiatric oncology. He practices at the St. Louis Cancer and Breast Institute and the Washington University School of Medicine. As the father of three girls, he works toward a society that encourages individuality, creativity and respect for the sacredness of everyday life.

Marty's photographs are on the following pages: 11, 24, 34, 44, 54, 55, 70, 76, 95, 98, 106, 108, 110, 114.

DAN DREYFUS is a professional photographer and owner of Dreyfus + Associates Photography in St. Louis. His work, which ranges from fine art to advertising, has appeared in numerous national and international publications. His recent book, *Reflections of Shaker Spirit*, a collaboration with Georgia Schmidt, won a number of local and national awards. Dan also teaches photography at Webster University. More of his work can be viewed online at dreyfusphoto.com.

Dan's photographs are on the following pages: Cover, 4, 6, 8, 18, 21, 26, 30, 32, 40, 48, 62, 78, 80, 90, 96, 101, 116.

Additional photo credits: Getty Images: 60; PictureQuest: 86, 92.